Be Brave To Be Fearless

by **Stacy Trimble**

Illustrations by **Mike Motz**

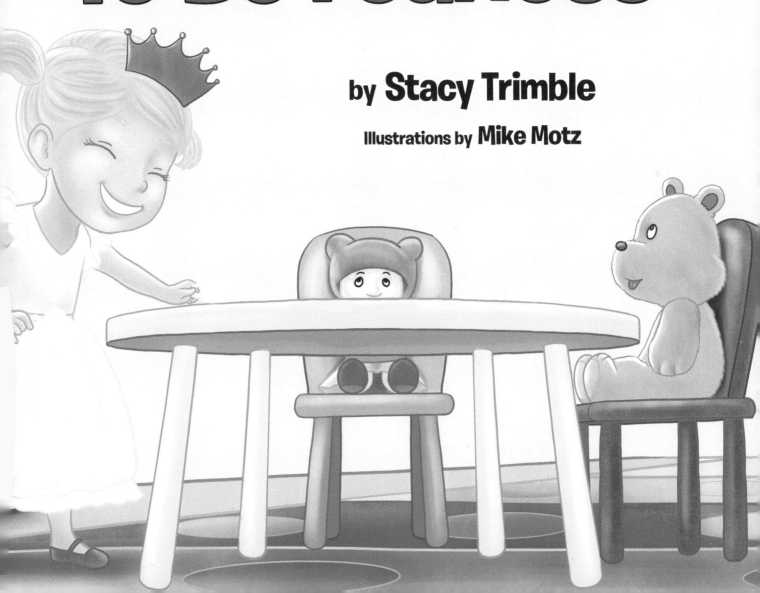

This book belongs to:

_____

Be Brave
To Be Fearless

Have you ever been faced with something that you feared? Something that you were afraid of?

Sometimes we have days that are scary, days that are painful, and moments where we just want to give up.

Those are the days we must stand up tall and fight.

We must always remember that God is bigger than the problems we face every day.

Every good and perfect
gift comes from above.
James 1:17

Austyn was the perfect combination of a princess and a warrior. She walked with such grace, always wearing that magical smile and believing in all the fairytales.

On the inside, Austyn was built with such strength, courage, and determination. She was everything her parents had prayed for.

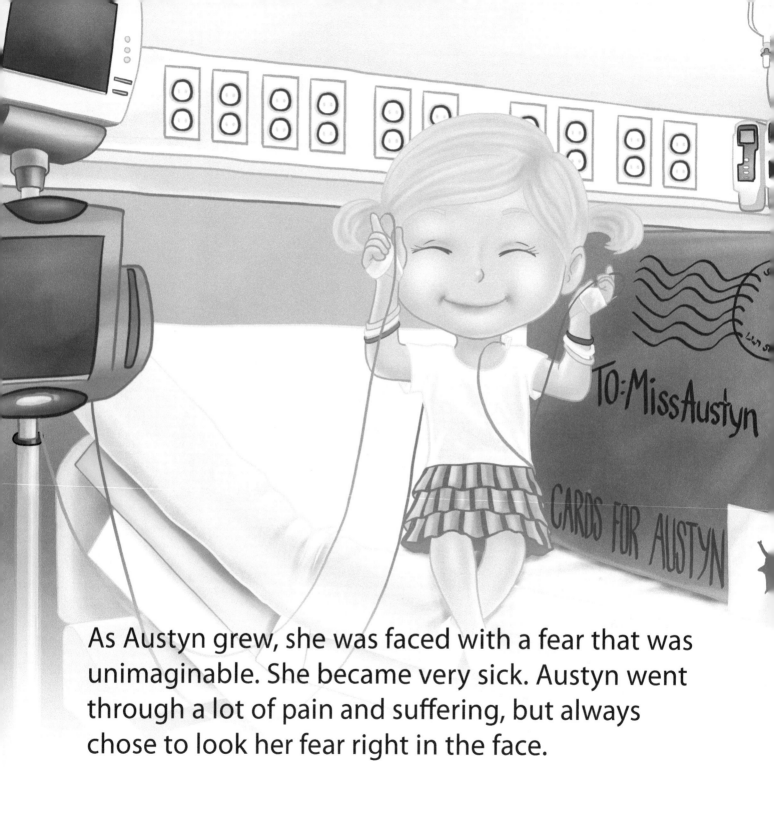

As Austyn grew, she was faced with a fear that was unimaginable. She became very sick. Austyn went through a lot of pain and suffering, but always chose to look her fear right in the face.

She is clothed in strength and dignity. Proverbs 31:25

Even when Austyn began to struggle, her faith continued to grow bigger. She always pushed forward, never giving up.

The Lord will fight for you; you need only to be still.
Exodus 14:14

God has a plan and purpose for each and every one of us. Sometimes we go through tough times to show others that it can be done.

God's plan for Austyn was just that. She taught everyone how to be fearless and that no matter what you are facing, you are strong and brave enough. You can and will overcome all the challenges and obstacles that you face every day.

As you fall down, always choose to get right back up.
Always believe in yourself, even when you feel your
strength is lost.

When you start to feel it's impossible, do not doubt God. Nothing is ever impossible with him.

Smile big, love hard, and enjoy every minute of life. Make memories, dream big, and never let fear take away your happiness.

Give thanks to the Lord,
for he is good. His love endures forever.
Psalm 136.1

Life is full of blessings. Embrace them, never letting anything stand in the way.

When those rough days decide to show up,
always remember...

You are brave, you are strong, and you are so loved.

Austyn is our shining star, breath of fresh air, and our strength when times get tough.

She is our warrior, always and forever.

About Austyn

Photo by Flair Photography

Austyn Halter was diagnosed with a rare form of leukemia, AML -M7 on August 17, 2015 at just 2 ½ years of age. She endured 6 rounds of chemotherapy at Texas Children's Hospital in Houston, Texas. After the 6th round, her leukemia worsened. Austyn was then accepted and flown to St. Jude Children's Research Hospital in Memphis, Tennessee on May 15, 2016 to take part in a research study. She received a HAPNK-1 stem cell transplant and celebrated her "new birthday" on June 9, 2016. Austyn was the 30th person ever to have this type of transplant. In the days ahead, she continued to fight against this horrible disease with such grace and never let it take away her joy. She smiled, she laughed, and she danced without fear. On August 4, 2017, she gained the most beautiful angel wings and received her miracle in Heaven. Throughout her journey, she was such an inspiration to others and touched so many lives. Austyn taught others to always fight and to never give up. She proved over and over that with faith, mountains could be moved. Austyn will always be remembered for her love, strength, courage, and desire to fight. She is missed beyond words but remains in our hearts, reminding us that nothing is impossible with God. #AustynStrong